BACKPACKER®
Winter
Camping
Skills

Molly Absolon

FALCONGUIDES

GUILFORD, CONNECTICUT
HELENA, MONTANA

In memory of AJ Linnell, who taught many of us the joys of winter adventures.

An imprint of Rowman & Littlefield

Backpacker is a registered trademark of Active Interest Media.
Falcon, FalconGuides, and Outfit Your Mind are registered trademarks of
Rowman & Littlefield.

Distributed by NATIONAL BOOK NETWORK

Copyright © 2016 by Rowman & Littlefield

British Library Cataloguing in Publication Information Available
Library of Congress Cataloging-in-Publication Data Available
ISBN 978-1-4930-1595-5 (paperback)
ISBN 978-1-4930-1596-2 (e-book)

♾™ The paper used in this publication meets the minimum requirements of
American National Standard for Information Sciences—Permanence of Paper for
Printed Library Materials, ANSI/NISO Z39.48-1992.

Contents

Snow is a perfect medium for play, be it skiing, sledding, or making snow angels. ALLEN O'BANNON

Introduction

Snow transforms the natural world. Surface hoar crystals glitter like diamonds scattered across the ground, catching the sun and creating rainbows on nature's white carpet. Piles of snow festoon the trees making them look like heads of cauliflower, lumpy, rounded, hiding the structures underneath. The color palette shifts to a muted one of whites, grays, browns, and blacks, varied only by occasional flashes of color from the sun that turn the white to pink or purple. In the absence of insects and birds, the world is strangely silent. Occasionally, you'll pass open water and hear a gurgling sound as it flows down under the ice, or perhaps, you'll be out when the snow is melting, and your background noise will be the constant drip of winter turning into spring. But more often the world around you is muffled, silent, and still.

Besides its beauty, winter can be fun. It's the one season where you can truly play. Snow allows you to build structures, forts, sculptures, and snowmen; you can slide down hills on skis, sleds, or snowboards and roll around to make snow angels.

But winter is also harsh. There's no denying that it takes hard work to stay comfortable and safe when the temperatures plummet and you are outside with no shelter. Staying warm, fed, and hydrated is a full-time job, even on days when the sun is shining. When

Winter transforms the world into a magical place. DON SHARAF

storms roll in and you have to contend with wind and snow, the workload escalates.

Still that workload does not have to be overwhelming. Once you have a system and know what you need to do, you'll find living outside in the winter can be comfortable and rewarding. That's where having some training comes in handy. Winter is an environment where it really behooves you to have a deep bag of tricks to make life easier.

So if winter camping appeals to you, prepare yourself. You'll be much happier with a little knowledge. Read this book. Take a course. Go out with more experienced friends. And start simple. Your first winter backpacking trip doesn't have to be a multi-day traverse of the Sierra Nevada. You can even try a night out in your backyard sometime to see what you think.

Chapter One

Choosing a Destination

Choosing an appropriate destination for your first—or your one-hundredth—winter trip can make the difference between a wonderful experience and an arduous misadventure. There are lots of factors that go into making this decision, including your experience level, your mode of transportation, your physical conditioning, and your time frame.

It doesn't take much to escape civilization in the winter. Less than a mile from a road, you can find yourself alone, wrapped in the silence of the winter world. So you don't have to be overly ambitious on your first excursion.

Ask yourself the following questions to help make your choice:

» Is this my first winter camping experience?
» What are my winter camping options in this area?
» Why do I want to go winter camping? Is my goal to interact with nature? Accomplish a specified objective like a peak climb or a traverse? Make turns?
» Do I want to spend most of my day traveling or base camping?
» Do I want to build a snow shelter?
» Do I understand the hazards?

Understanding your skill level and goals will help you choose an appropriate destination for your winter camping trip. ALLEN O'BANNON

These kinds of questions will help you narrow down your options. If your goal is to ski downhill, your best bet may be to make a base camp from which you can venture out on day tours. If you are on snowshoes and your plan is to climb a peak, you may move your camp every day to set yourself up for an attempt on

Winter transforms your surroundings into a whole new world.
THINKSTOCK.COM, WOJCIECH GAJDA

the summit. If you want to sleep in a snow shelter, you may choose to go a quarter mile from the road to dig in.

This book will go into hazards in detail later, but it's worth thinking about what can hurt, maim, or kill you when you are looking for a place to go. The primary concerns for a winter traveler include cold temperatures, open water or dangerous ice, and avalanches. Look at a map or ask around at local gear shops or in online forums to find out what hazards you need to be prepared for before you venture out to your chosen destination. Check the weather. Be conservative, especially as you are gaining experience.

HOW FAR CAN YOU GO?

Travel in winter can be more time consuming than it is in the summer. Your speed will be highly variable and depends on your mode of transportation, whether you are breaking trail or following a groomed route, and the amount of gear you are carrying. It's easy to

Breaking trail through deep powder is arduous and slow, so allow extra time in your schedule if you intend to venture off the beaten path. ALLEN O'BANNON

move rapidly downhill in the right snow conditions. In fact, you may find that a mountain that took you five hours to climb takes one hour to descend if you are on skis or glissading on a firm surface. All these variables make it very hard to put a figure to the number of miles you can expect to travel on any given day.

In the summer, most people hiking with a pack on a trail average 2 to 3 miles per hour and can easily cover 5 to 10 miles a day or more. In the winter, if you expect to break trail, halve the distance you'd go on a summer trip for your first excursion. If you plan to be on a well-broken trail, your pace will probably be closer to your summer pace, but things will still take longer. You have to add and subtract layers of clothing to stay at a comfortable temperature; you need to eat more than normal to keep your energy up. You've got more stuff to deal with, setting up camp takes longer, and going to the bathroom can be a full-on expedition, so even if your travel pace is close to your summer pace, start off conservatively and give yourself plenty of time. Remember, winter days are shorter too.

Keep track of how long things take on your first few excursions to get a sense of your travel speed. Make note of conditions, so you can factor that in the next time you head out. Snow is a lot more variable than a summer trail. So pay attention. The knowledge you accumulate over time will better prepare you for your next trip.

Beginner Tip: For your first winter camping trip, choose a location that is about one mile from the road and set up a base camp from which you can explore farther.

Snow Conditions

The condition of the snow is the number one factor in determining your travel speed. Snow comes in all shapes and textures. What falls from the sky is very different from what lies on the ground a week after the storm. Temperature, moisture, wind, aspect, and time all affect snow conditions. You may find yourself wallowing in sugary faceted snow where you punch all the way to the ground, or you may be able to walk across a frozen crust that supports your weight and makes the going easy.

Snow comes in all shapes and textures, which affects how fast you can travel. Sastrugi, which is carved by the wind, is often firm so you can move on top without breaking through, but its uneven surface can make for slow going. DON SHARAF

The only way to predict what kind of conditions you can expect to encounter is by paying attention to the weather and having a basic understanding of snow metamorphism. In simple terms, long, cold, dry spells transform snow into unconsolidated faceted grains that make travel hard. Think floundering in deep, loose sand. On the other hand, warm days, cold nights, or solar radiation can create a frozen crust that is good for travel in the morning, yet more challenging in the afternoon, as the snow loses its ability to support your weight when the crust melts. Temperatures in the teens and 20s that stay consistent tend to create a strong, well-bonded snowpack that is good for travel.

Beginner Tip: Make your first trip a few days after a snowfall and during a period when no storms are in the forecast.

Temperature

When choosing a destination, it is helpful to know the temperatures you are likely to encounter to ensure you are well-prepared. You can visit weather websites to determine averages and extremes for the area you plan to visit. You can talk to locals about the conditions you should expect to find. And you can choose your season to correspond to your goals.

Winter means cold, but if you have the right clothes, food, and equipment, you can stay happy and warm regardless.
ALLEN O'BANNON

Beginner Tip: Pick a destination where you can expect temperatures in the teens and 20s. Too much colder and camping becomes more challenging. Too much warmer and you'll find yourself struggling to keep dry.

Terrain

For many winter travelers, terrain is the determining factor in choosing a destination. Whether you prefer powder skiing or ice fishing will play a huge role in deciding where to go. Winter peak ascents have added challenge, and forests are transformed

In the winter, snow covers obstacles that otherwise make off-trail travel challenging, so you can go just about anywhere. DON SHARAF

by winter into a magical place to explore. Snow can make going off trail easier than in the summer when vegetation and deadfall can make it difficult to hike through the woods.

If you plan to travel on foot without snowshoes, look for open, windswept, or south-facing slopes where snow levels are minimal, making travel easier. Snowshoers do best on flat or gently rolling terrain, although more experienced snowshoers can tackle steep slopes with mountaineering-style snowshoes. Downhill skiers are going to want open slopes or widely spaced trees to carve turns through. Certain activities require groomed trails, such as skate skiing or skijoring, which will direct you to specific destinations and terrain.

Beginner Tip: Pick your destination based on your goals. Talk to local experts, consult guidebooks and the Internet, or consider hiring a guide for your first excursion to ensure you choose a place that will satisfy your objectives without subjecting you to undue hardship or danger.

WHEN TO GO?

In general, early season (meaning late fall and early winter) means less snow on the ground, which can make travel easier, especially if you plan to be on foot. However, the days are also short and the temperatures can be brutally cold.

Midwinter means a more consolidated snowpack, but you'll still have short days and cold temperatures.

Late winter, early spring is characterized by more melting and freezing, resulting in variable snow conditions. Travel in the morning can be easy if the snow surface is frozen. Later in the day, conditions can change dramatically as things heat up. But the days are long, and the temperatures more moderate than earlier in the year.

Often late-season winter travel is easy in the early part of the day when the snow surface is frozen and will support your weight.
MOLLY ABSOLON

Chapter Two

Winter Camping Equipment

Winter is the one season where your gear really makes a difference between comfort and misery, or even survival. So it's important to pack carefully and know how to use your equipment before you head out into freezing temperatures.

CLOTHING

As a species, humans evolved in hot climates. We moved into colder parts of the planet thousands of years ago, but our bodies have been slow to adapt. We have not developed the dense, insulating fur or blubbery fat of cold-adapted animals, nor are we likely to do so. To compensate for this lack of physiological traits, we have to use our brains and rely on clothing, food, and shelter.

We generate heat through metabolism (the transformation of food into usable energy) and exercise. Exercise can produce fifteen to eighteen times as much heat as metabolism, so when you are outdoors, exercise is going to be a major source of quick heat. But you need to fuel the fire, so food is also critical to staying warm.

Humans lose heat through evaporation, conduction, convection, and radiation. It's helpful to

To be comfortable in the winter, you need to constantly adjust your clothing. Things like wearing hats, booties, wind gear, and neckwarmers and standing or sitting on some kind of pad are a few of the easy things you can do to stay warm. ALLEN O'BANNON

understand these principles, as they can dictate how you dress appropriately for conditions.

Evaporation of sweat or water cools your skin. A wet surface, like your skin, loses heat twenty-five times faster than a dry one. When it's hot out, this is an excellent way to stay cool. Obviously, when it's cold out that can be a problem. The key to preventing heat loss from evaporation in the winter is to stay dry. That means adding and subtracting clothing to keep you from overheating as you exercise, and wearing waterproof clothing when it's stormy.

Conduction is the transfer of heat from a warm body to a cold one in an attempt to reach a common temperature. What that means for you, as you tromp around at 98.6°F, is that everything you touch will be stealing your precious body heat. To avoid the loss of heat through conduction, you need to insulate yourself from the cold around you. Stand on a pad while you cook, wear mittens or gloves when you handle objects, and sit on a pack or pad to stay off the snow.

Convection is the loss of heat through the movement of air or liquid. In the winter, that loss is typically a result of the wind. The rate of heat loss through convection is directly proportional to the difference in temperature between you and your surroundings, hence the reason the wind chill factor makes the air

Convection is the loss of heat through the movement of air or liquid. The rate of convective loss is directly proportional to the difference between you and your surroundings; so cold, windy days feel particularly chilly. Good wind gear helps minimize convective heat loss. MOLLY ABSOLON

feel a lot colder than it is. To prevent convective heat loss, you need to wear windproof clothing.

Radiation is the heat given off as a by-product of your basal metabolism. The goal in winter is to trap that heat rather than let it escape (except if you are exercising and getting sweaty). The best way to trap this heat is by layering clothing to create dead air space around your body, where the heat can be captured.

Dressing for Conditions

You'll find in the winter that you are constantly putting on and taking off clothing to regulate your temperature. When you are moving, you may wear little more than a base layer and wind gear, but the minute you stop you'll need to throw on a parka.

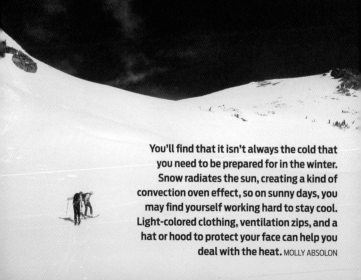

You'll find that it isn't always the cold that you need to be prepared for in the winter. Snow radiates the sun, creating a kind of convection oven effect, so on sunny days, you may find yourself working hard to stay cool. Light-colored clothing, ventilation zips, and a hat or hood to protect your face can help you deal with the heat. MOLLY ABSOLON

Generally, people feel the cold first in their extremities. That's because, as our bodies cool down, our brain shunts the blood back to our core, where the organs critical to life reside. We can survive without fingers and toes, but we don't want to. So that means you need to pay attention to your hands and feet and work to keep them warm.

On the trail, it's nice to have some quick, easy accessory items to slip on or off as the temperatures change. This includes things like a hat, mittens or heavier gloves, a neck warmer or balaclava, and a wind shirt. Changing into dry socks can also help with cold toes.

Materials

There are all sorts of materials for outdoor clothing out there, and companies are coming up with new stuff all the time. Today's technical clothing comes in wool, nylon, down, polypropylene, and so forth. You can even find clothing with battery-operated heaters for extreme temperatures.

When determining the appropriate materials, you want to bear in mind the ways humans lose heat and make sure your clothing can withstand these vectors. So you need windproof, waterproof, insulated clothing.

Most of today's outdoor gear is designed for these uses, so rather than dictate any one particular fabric, here are some general guidelines to help you narrow down your choices:

- » **Cotton:** This has no real place out in the winter except for a bandana to clean your sunglasses. Cotton holds moisture, so if you sweat in cotton, you end up wet and cold.
- » **Capilene/Polypropylene:** These types of fabrics wick away moisture, maintain insulating capability when wet, and dry quickly. They are used for base layers and in thicker weights for insulation.
- » **Wool:** Wool retains its insulating capacity when wet, and it is less likely to retain odors than synthetics like polypropylene. High-end wool clothing can be expensive, and some people find it itchy (although the newer merino wools seem to have fixed that problem for most folks). Wool sweaters work well as insulating layers, but can be bulky for packing and take longer to dry than most synthetics.
- » **Down:** Down is lightweight, compressible, and very warm, unless it gets wet—in which case it turns into a useless rag. Down is an excellent choice for a winter parka or insulated pants if you live in a relatively dry climate such as the Rocky Mountains. If you think you are going to have trouble keeping dry, opt for a synthetic parka or select a water-resistant down parka.
- » **Synthetic Fillings:** Modern synthetic fillings are much better than they used to be in terms

Basic Winter Clothing List

Upper Body

- » 2 base layers; one lightweight top that will be like your skin, and one expedition weight layer (Zipped turtleneck tops allow you some venting capability and help keep your neck warm.)
- » 1 insulating layer (down or synthetic parka)
- » For overnight trips, you probably want to include one more layer, such as a pile jacket or a big winter parka.
- » 1 waterproof, breathable, windproof storm jacket with hood

Bottom Layers

- » 1 pair base layer long underwear
- » 1 pair water-resistant, windproof storm pants (Gore-Tex or soft shell)
- » For overnight trips, bring a pair of insulated pants.

Feet

- » 2–4 pairs of socks (The key is to have an extra pair of dry socks available to wear around camp and for sleeping—these socks should never get wet.)

of weight and compressibility. Now you can get jackets that will pack down to a small size and are quite light. They probably are never going to be quite as good as down on these fronts, but they have the benefit of maintaining their

» Gaiters (These are essential to keep snow out of your boots. Most ski pants come with built-in gaiters. Make sure these stay down securely around your boot.)

» Bootie system (For overnight trips, you'll want to have some kind of bootie system that allows you to take off your boots in camp. An insulated bootie with a sole works great, or if you have plastic boots with removable liners, you can pull out the liners, put in an insole, and wear insulated, soleless booties inside the plastic shells to walk around camp.)

Hands

» 2 pairs of gloves (Liner type gloves are prefereable. Wool is nice because you can handle hot things in the kitchen, and they tend to keep you a bit warmer when they get damp.)

» 1 pair of insulated mittens or gloves

Head

» Make sure your insulated parka has a hood.

» 1 wool hat

» 1 neckwarmer, Buff headwear, or balaclava

insulating capacity when they are wet, so if you live in a place where the temperatures hover around freezing and you could get rain or wet snow, synthetic fillings are best and are usually cheaper than down.

Helpful Hints

» Zipper pulls made from parachute cord or duct tape make life easier in the winter, as most of the time you will be wearing mittens or gloves when you need to manipulate your zipper.

» Pack your water bottle in a sock or an insulated bootie to keep it from freezing.

» Carry a small insulated bottle for tea or hot chocolate on the trail.

» Put a small hot-water bottle (1/2 liter size) in your pocket or sleeping bag for a cozy external heat source (make sure the lid is on firmly).

PACKS, SLEDS, AND WINTER ESSENTIALS

Camping has undergone a lightweight revolution in the past ten to fifteen years. These principles apply to winter camping and can help you lighten your load, but you'll still be a bit more burdened than in the summer just because of all the stuff you need to stay comfortable camping in the snow. That said, bear in mind that the materials used to construct your gear can add unnecessary pounds to your load. You don't need a bulletproof backpack. Buy gear and clothing made from lightweight material with a minimum of extra whistles and bells to keep weight down.

Packs

There are endless options for backpacks on the market. When narrowing down your choices, consider the following:

Ease of access: When you are wearing mittens or gloves, lots of straps and buckles and zippers can be a pain. It's nice to have an easy way into your pack that you can access without having to remove your gloves. Some packs have a "clamshell" opening in the back that you can unzip to get into the main body of the pack; others have a side zipper to allow access. Such features are nice in the winter.

When you are wearing gloves or mittens, lots of zippers and buckles are hard to manage. Backpacks with some kind of easy access, like this clamshell opening in the back, allow you to get to your stuff quickly with minimal clipping and zipping. MOLLY ABSOLON

Backpack Fitting

Having a backpack that fits well is critical to your comfort. Your best bet for securing a good fit is to buy from a reputable dealer who can help you find a pack well-suited to your body.

When you try on a pack, run through the following steps to ensure it's adjusted properly for your frame:

Loosen all the straps. Then place the pack on your back and tighten the hip belt. The padded part of the hip belt should fit on top of your hipbones. Make sure that you have an inch or two of space on either side of the hip belt buckle, so you can make adjustments as you add and subtract layers.

Snug down the shoulder straps so they wrap around your shoulders. The anchor point of the straps should fall an inch or two below the top of your shoulder.

Many packs have load-lifter straps on top of the shoulder straps. Tighten these once you have secured your shoulder straps. The load-lifter straps should go back to the pack at a 45-degree angle and lift the weight up off your shoulders.

Finally, if the pack has stabilizer straps that attach to the outside of the hip belt, snug these down last. These straps pull the pack body close to the hip belt and stabilize your load.

Load the pack up when you try it on, so you can get a sense of how it will carry weight. When you are skiing or snowshoeing with a pack, it's nice to have one that rides close to your body and moves with you, so you don't get thrown off balance. Most stores will have sandbags or something you can use to test out a backpack's feel.

Size: Winter packs need to be large enough to carry bulky clothes, food, and water, in addition to a shovel and probe if you intend to travel in avalanche country. The size is determined by the amount of time you intend to be out and the hazards you might encounter. Make sure you have enough space. Leaving critical items behind can be a safety hazard, and it can be annoying to deal with an overstuffed pack in the cold. For a three- or four-night trip, you should look for a pack that will hold 65 to 80 liters; smaller if you are going light; bigger if you want to bring a few extras.

Features: Often the straps, loops, and pockets added to backpacks just get in the way and add weight. So think about your goals when determining the extra features you'll need. You may want a way to straps skis, a snowboard, or snowshoes onto your pack. You may need an ice ax loop or a shovel pocket. But don't be sold on too many special features if you don't need them. They often just go unused.

Sleds

You will have to carry a lot more weight in the winter than you do in the summer. Most winter diets contain roughly twice as many calories as a summer ration, and you'll need extra fuel in the winter to melt snow into water. Plus, there's the extra clothing and equipment you need to be comfortable. Carrying all this gear on your back is cumbersome and awkward, so

For multiday trips, a sled made for hauling a load is invaluable. The rigid poles allow for better control and maneuverability in varied terrain. DON SHARAF

having a sled to spread out the weight on multiday trips is helpful.

You can rig up a sled by adding extra straps to a cheap plastic sled, or you can buy an expensive sled with metal bars and a waist harness. These sleds are preferable if you intend to be out for a long time and expect to do a lot of winter camping because the rigid poles make them more maneuverable.

Kiddie sleds are usually pulled with a rope attached to the sled and tied to your hip belt. This works fine when you are moving forward in a straight line over level terrain or up gentle climbs. They become a bit of a nuisance when you are side-hilling, as the sleds tend to slip out of the track and drag below you, and they can be tricky when you are descending, as they usually pass you by and pull you downhill. But they work and can help you carry extra gear for short trips.

Winter Essentials

Shovel: A snow shovel is a critical piece of winter gear. You'll use it to create a shelter, collect snow for melting water, dig pits to analyze the snow conditions, and, in an emergency, dig your friends out of an avalanche. You need a shovel that is designed for winter use, not a garden spade you pick up in a hardware store. Buy one with a detachable, extendable handle for ease in packing and to save your back when you are digging.

Saw: Snow saws can be useful for cutting blocks when building snow shelters or for conducting tests in snow pits to analyze the snowpack. Lightweight, aluminum saws specially designed for winter use are preferable.

A saw designed for cutting snow is a useful tool for making blocks to build your shelter or kitchen and for snow tests to determine avalanche conditions. MOLLY ABSOLON

Avalanche safety gear: Depending on your location, route, and chosen activity, you may need to be prepared for avalanches. Basic avalanche safety equipment includes a transceiver, probe, and shovel. Battery-operated transceivers transmit or receive a signal, so you can pinpoint someone buried in an avalanche. Probes help with searching as well, and can cut down the time it takes to locate a victim. This gear is only useful if you know how to use it. If you plan to be in avalanche terrain, get training.

SHELTERS

Tents

Tents are the simplest, fastest, and most convenient winter shelter. You just need to stomp out a level platform, set up your tent, and you are good to go. If you want, you can dig a trench in front of the door, so you can sit with your feet dangling down to take off your boots before moving inside, but that is not necessary. It just makes it easier to keep snow out of your tent.

You need to make sure that your tent is intended for four-season use with poles that are strong enough to withstand a snow load and that you have enough guy lines to secure the tent firmly in the snow.

The only downside to tents is that they tend to be heavy, and they aren't as warm as a snow shelter (or as quiet in a storm for that matter). But nothing beats the ease of throwing up a tent and crawling into bed.

Tents are the simplest, fastest winter shelter. You just need to stomp out a platform, and up they go. But tents are not as warm as snow shelters, and in windy, exposed spots, it's nice to build snow walls for protection. SARAH CARPENTER

Tarps

Tarps can actually work quite well in the winter. You can use a pyramid-style tarp, such as the Black

With tarps, you can dig down into the snow to make more room. This tarp is being used as a gathering place for a group to escape wintery conditions outside. SARAH CARPENTER

Diamond Megamid, or an A-line, roof-style tarp, strung between two trees. Most of the pyramid-style tarps come with a central pole. You'll need to put a pad under the pole to keep it from punching through the snow, or you can hang the tarp from a tree branch and forgo the pole all together.

Floorless shelters work best if you stomp out a platform and then build walls around the edges to close in the space and create a cozy, roomy sleeping area. Make sure the tarp extends over the outside of the wall so that snow can slide off rather than down into your shelter. You may want to bring a ground cloth to cover the floor of your shelter and keep yourself up off the snow.

Deadmen

The best way to secure your tent or tarp down in the winter is either with a snow stake or a deadman. Snow stakes are useful in the Arctic where the snowpack is shallow and sugary and you expect fierce winds. For the continental United States, you can just use deadmen. To make your deadmen, gather up a bunch of sticks about 6 inches long and thumb thick. You'll need as many sticks as you have guy lines to secure.

Dig a trench about 8–10 inches deep at a right angle to the guy line's attachment point. Place the guy line across the trench and put a stick on top (a). Push the stick to the bottom of the trench and bury it with snow, making sure to keep the guy line free. Stamp on the snow and give it a couple of minutes to set (b). Once the snow is firm, pull the guy line and tie it off to your shelter the way you would with a tent stake (c). You may need to run the string back and forth a bit to free it up, so you can make adjustments. When you leave, there's no need to dig up the stick. Just pull the string out and off you go.

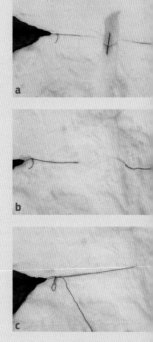

MOLLY ABSOLON

Snow Shelters

We'll have a whole section on snow shelters, but here is a plug for them now. If you are into winter camp-

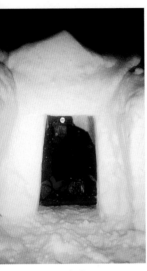

ing, you should sleep in a snow shelter at least once in your life. There's nothing quite like being tucked in your own cozy cave, out of the wind, away from the roar of a storm, reading by candlelight. It's great. Snow shelters take a lot of work—several hours usually—but they are wonderful inside. It can be raging outside with high winds, bitter cold temperatures, and lots of snow, and you can be sitting in a balmy 30°F with no sound at all. To build a snow shelter, you'll need a shovel and possibly a saw if you want to cut blocks. Read more about snow shelters in chapter 3.

Snow shelters protect you from the wind, cold, and snow and provide you with a cozy place to sleep and hang out away from the challenges of winter. ALLEN O'BANNON

Yurts and Huts

Finally, in many mountainous parts of the world, there are alpine huts and yurts that you can stay in during the winter. Some of these shelters are little more than a lean-to that will get you out of the wind; others have wood stoves, beds, outhouses or toilets, saunas—the works. These shelters can be a great way to get out and enjoy the winter environment with a little more luxury in your accommodations.

CAMPING EQUIPMENT

Stoves: In cold temperatures, white gas stoves tend to work better than stoves that use a cartridge of compressed butane and propane. It has to do with the chemistry of these fuels and the way they react to cold. Butane stops vaporizing at warmer temperatures than propane (around 31ºF), which means the propane will burn off more rapidly than the butane. As you are left with more butane, you have less vapor pressure inside the canister and end up with a weak, sputtering flame that makes cooking slow and tedious. There have been some advances in stove technology, and you may find a blended fuel canister designed for colder temperatures, but in general white gas stoves are more reliable for winter camping. That said, if the temperatures get down around −30ºF, you can expect any stove to be fussy and difficult. Rubber parts get hard and shrink, making it difficult to maintain seals, and liquid fuel is slow to vaporize, making it hard to prime your stove. The stoves will work; you just need to be patient.

Practice with your stove outside in the cold at home just to make sure it works. Fixing a stove in cold temperatures can be difficult and frustrating.

If you have three or more people on your trip and you know you will have to melt snow for water, you probably will want to bring two stoves. One stove will be in almost continuous use, making water; the other can be used for preparing food.

You will need to carry a stove pad with you in the winter to keep your stove from melting down into the snow. You can buy special stove pads designed for this purpose (remember if your stove pad is made from metal, it will heat up and melt in, so you'll need to insulate it), or you can make one with a piece of plywood. You may also want a pad to put your warm pot on to keep it from sinking into the snow.

Lanterns: Winter days are short, especially in December and January, so it's nice to have a lantern. A small candle, white gas, or battery-powered lantern works great and can add some homey cheer to your dark campsite. Remember: don't take gas lanterns or stoves into your snow shelter. The airflow inside most snow caves or quinzhees is not sufficient to prevent carbon monoxide poisoning, so beware. On the other hand, candle or battery-powered lanterns work fine inside.

Fuel: In the winter, it is often difficult to get to running water. Everything is frozen, which means you may have to melt snow for water, and that means you

It's nice to bring a lantern along in the winter since the days are short and nights are long. AJ LINNELL

will need more fuel in the winter than you do in the summer. Typically, in the summer, a group of three uses about one-third a liter or less of fuel a day (in a white gas stove), depending on what kind of food you are cooking. In the winter, the same group may use up to three-fourth a liter of fuel per day, mainly because of the amount required to melt snow. So calculate your amounts accordingly and keep track of how much you use when you are out there, so you can fine tune your amounts for your next trip.

Pots, skillet, utensils: In general, you can plan on bringing the same cooking gear you bring on your summer outings in the winter. However, because you need to melt snow for drinking water, it's a good idea to have two big pots.

SLEEPING SYSTEMS

Sleeping bag: You need a bag that is rated to the temperature extremes you expect to encounter. In many parts of the country, this means a bag rated to −20°F or −30°F. Take into consideration your own body temperature. Knowing you sleep hot or cold can help you decide what temperature rating to go for. If you are just starting out, a good bet is to carry a bag that is rated for 10°F below the coldest temperature you expect.

Sleeping pads: Having a full-length, thick inflatable pad for sleeping is great. These days there are pads specifically designed to be used in cold temperatures. Ask for guidance when you go shopping or do some research online to determine what brands provide the most insulation. You can find insulated inflatable pads on the market that are a nice luxury when camping on snow. Be sure to carry a repair kit in case your pad goes flat. In addition, it's a good idea to carry a half-pad made from some kind of insulating foam. This pad can be used to sit and stand on around camp and then can go under your full-length pad to provide an extra buffer against conduction when you lie down on the snow to go to sleep.

PERSONAL ITEMS

Flashlight and extra batteries: Headlamps are nice so that you can have your hands free when working in the dark. Lithium batteries tend to last longer in the cold.

Toiletries: What you bring depends on your personal habits, but remember liquids will freeze in your pack. If you wear contacts and need to bring solution, bring the minimum amount you require and carry it in a pocket or pouch against your body to keep it from freezing. Otherwise, bring a toothbrush, a small amount of toothpaste, sunscreen (sunscreen sticks are nice as you don't need to worry about freezing), and lip balm.

Sunglasses and goggles: You will probably want both glasses and goggles in the winter. Goggles are critical in a storm, and sunglasses are necessary on bright sunny days when the glare off the snow can burn your corneas, causing snow blindness. It's nice to have a cotton bandana or cloth to use on your goggles when they get wet or fogged up. On ascents, you can stuff the cloth inside the goggles to keep them clear until you want to put them on again.

Water bottles and insulated bottles: You need to make a conscious effort to stay hydrated in the winter, so consider bringing a thermos along for hot tea during the day. Water bottles with wide mouths are best for winter camping, as they are easier to fill. Keep your water bottle insulated in a bootie or wrapped in a coat inside your pack, so the water doesn't freeze.

Pee bottle: A wide-mouth Nalgene bottle or bowl with a screw-top lid works great as a pee bottle. You may think gross, but before ruling it out, give it a try. You'll spend long hours in bed in the winter, and, inevitably, you'll have to pee before it's time to get up. Having a pee bottle keeps you from having to get into your clothes and put on boots to go outside your shelter. That said, there are definitely stories of spilled pee bottles, and, for women, it may take a little practice if you've never used one before. Make sure the lid is screwed on tightly after you are done. And check the volume. You don't want to overflow the bottle in the middle of the night. Finally, mark your bottle so you don't inadvertently use it for drinking water.

REPAIR KITS

It's important to be able to fix your gear in the field. You will want to bring along a repair kit for your skis or snowshoes, one for camping equipment such as shelters and stoves, and a first aid kit.

Chapter Three

Living in the Snow

One of the best things about winter camping is creating your campsite. You can build a veritable town in the snow: houses, walls, paths, seats—you name it, you can create it with a little ingenuity and some shoveling.

ARRIVING IN CAMP

When you arrive in camp the first thing you should do is put on layers. Your body is warm from exercise, and you want to capture that heat to keep from chilling down when you stop moving. You may also want to put on dry socks right away. Again, it's a preventative measure to ensure you don't get cold. It's a lot harder to warm up in the winter than it is to stay warm, so it's best to avoid that challenge.

CAMPSITE SELECTION

Look for a campsite that is out of the bottom of a valley or drainage since cold air sinks, making these spots chillier than a nearby site on top of a hill. Think about sunlight and whether you prefer morning or evening sun. It's nice to position yourself so that you can benefit from its warming effects at some time during the day.

Unlike summer camping, you don't have to think about access to water when you choose your site, and you can level the area with a shovel, so you can camp just about anywhere. It's nice to have protection from the wind, so tuck in behind some trees or use the surrounding topography to escape its full blast.

Look at the surrounding terrain before you commit to a site. Don't plop yourself down in a meadow below a steep slope, or you may find yourself in the runout zone of an avalanche.

CHORES

Winter camping requires a lot of work, so it's most fun and efficient when everyone in your group pitches in to get things done. The list of things that need to be completed to establish your camp include: building a shelter or erecting your tent, lighting a stove to get water and food started, digging out a kitchen, organizing your gear so that things don't get lost in the snow, and taking care of yourself so you don't get cold.

Divvy up these tasks and rotate through them during your trip, so one person isn't always in charge of cooking or building the kitchen.

Make sure you stay organized as you explode your packs, change your clothes, and build your camp. Gear can disappear quickly in the snow, especially once you start digging. Try to keep everything in a duffel, your backpack, or your shelter. The fewer places you have to look for things, the easier it will be to find them if you get a foot of snow overnight.

SNOW SHELTERS

There are a number of different shelters you can build out of snow. The type you choose will be determined by snow conditions, time, and group size.

Snow Caves

Snow caves are relatively simple if you can find a big drift. To determine if your drift is of adequate size, pull

There are a lot of chores that need to be completed to ensure you have a safe, comfortable winter camp. You'll find it works best to divvy up tasks so that everything gets done. AJ LINNELL

out your probe and poke around to see how much snow you have to work with. Depending on how many people you want to shelter, you'll need at least a 6-foot drift. Once you've found a good location,

Work-Hardening Snow

If you have ever made a snowball, you'll understand work hardening. When snow is warm and under pressure it changes; the crystals round and break down and bond more easily together. Some snow, especially warm snow in relatively mild conditions, work hardens readily. Other types, such as the sugary snow found in cold, dry climates, takes a lot of work to get it to stick together.

Your ultimate structure will determine the specifics of how you will proceed, but the general process of work-hardening snow is to stomp out a platform for your shelter or kitchen with your skis or snowshoes on, then stomp again in your boots to create a firm floor. Once you have your foundation, mound up piles of snow, smacking it with a shovel as your pile grows. When your mound is of sufficient size for whatever you intend to build, let it sit. The length of time required depends on your snow type. With really sugary snow, you may need to let it sit overnight, warmer snow may take less than an hour. You can tell your pile is ready to go if you carve out well-bonded chunks when you dig, rather than having the snow collapse in a pile of fluff around you.

start digging following the general principles of snow shelter construction listed in the following pages.

Quinzhees

Quinzhee is an Athabaskan Indian word for a snow shelter made from piling up snow and then hollowing it out—essentially creating your own snow drift. The Athabaskans lived in the interior of Canada, in extremely cold, dry climates where there

Snow shelters take time and a lot of work to construct, but the result is a comfortable home that will last for days. DON SHARAF

wasn't much snow, so they developed this technique to take advantage of what little they had.

To build a quinzhee, start by work hardening your base. A good technique for determining the basic shape and size of your quinzhee is to have one person on skis stand and step around in a circle, keeping the tails of his or her skis in place at a center point. This circle will give you enough space for a quinzhee that sleeps three. If you need more room, make your circle bigger.

After you've designated your shape, remove your skis and boot pack around the perimeter of your circle. This will be the foundation for your walls. You'll

To help speed up the excavation process, you can pile up the snow over big duffel bags. When you start digging out the inside, you can pull out the bags to create more space inside. Just remember not to put anything in the bags that you might need during the construction process. Stick ski poles and skis into your pile to give the mole an indication of thickness as she or he excavates the interior of your shelter. ALLEN O'BANNON

want the foundation to be a minimum of 18 inches thick. Mark the perimeter with skis or poles so that you know where it is when you start digging.

Once the foundation is established, you can throw a couple of large zip bags or backpacks into the center of your circle to take up some space, so you don't have to pile up and remove as much snow as you create your shelter. Remember you may not be able to get into these bags for a few hours, so don't put anything critical inside.

Now start piling on the snow. Your goal is to create a giant gumdrop that rises well over head-height. This takes a long time and a lot of snow, so be prepared. When your mound is the correct size, smack it with your shovels to accelerate the work hardening and help smooth out the walls. Walk around the

Your completed snow shelter will look a little bit like a gumdrop in its shape. ALLEN O'BANNON

perimeter to see if there are any flat places or spots that need more snow. Once you are satisfied with the shape and size, let the mound rest for a least a half an hour in good conditions. In marginal conditions, you may want to go for a ski for a couple of hours or even sleep in a tent overnight to let the mound set.

The final step is to dig out the inside, following the general principles listed below.

MOLING OUT YOUR SHELTER

The individual assigned to dig out the interior of your shelter is called the mole for obvious reasons. When it's time to begin digging, the mole should strip down to long underwear and wind gear and anticipate getting wet. It's a good idea to save dry clothes to change into after the shelter is complete. The mole begins by excavating a door and then tunneling back for a couple of feet before creating a sleeping chamber. It helps to shorten the handle on your shovel when you first begin moling. As you create space, you can lengthen the handle again.

In general, carve out your snow shelter by shaving away the snow in an arcing motion that leaves all open spaces with a curving roof. Remember, an arch is the strongest shape in nature and, therefore, will hold up longer and be less likely to collapse than a shelter with a flat roof.

A finished snow shelter is extremely strong. Most sag rather than collapse with age. But when you are digging the shelter out, there is a chance it can fail and fall down, pinning the mole inside. This is rare, unless your snow is not adequately work hardened or your mole forgets to create arcing spaces. Regardless, because of the potential for collapse, a mole should never be left unattended. Have a second person stand by the door, moving snow away as the mole pushes it out from inside.

You can provide guides for the mole by sticking probes, ski poles, and skis about 18 inches into the mound of snow. When the mole hits one of these markers, he or she will have reached the desired thickness of the wall.

In cold temperatures, and when you have a deep enough snowpack, it's nice to create a kind of airlock in your shelter to stay warmer inside. To do this, have the mole tunnel back 2 feet and then begin digging upward to hollow out your sleeping chamber, keeping the floor level about a foot or so above the floor level of the tunnel. To help you picture the end result, imagine it's like a step leading up into your bedroom from the hallway.

Once you have the shape and size you want, smooth out the floor and poke a few holes through the walls to allow some ventilation. You'll be amazed how hot and humid it can get inside if you don't allow a little airflow.

The snow you excavate from inside your shelter can be used to make a snow kitchen or even a kitchen quinzhee, so think about where you want to pile it up as you move it away from the door. Kitchen quinzhees need lots of ventilation to be safe for cooking, so make sure you build them with a big door and air holes.

Finish the shelter off by carving out alcoves for candles or shelves for your belongings.

DIGLOOS

A digloo is either a snow cave or a quinzhee with a capped roof. With this type of shelter, two people can dig it out at the same time: one through the door, the other through a hole in the middle of the roof. Once the two diggers meet in the middle, you can create a cap using blocks of snow to enclose the space.

If you opt to build a digloo, create a quarry for your blocks. Stamp out an area about a ski-length long and a ski pole-length wide. Let the quarry sit while you work on your snow shelter. Then when you are

Snow blocks for capping shelters or creating wind walls can be created by cutting blocks out of a work-hardened snow quarry. DON SHARAF

ready, cut blocks that are approximately 20 inches long, 5 inches thick, and about 14 inches high. These blocks are big enough that you won't have to use a ton to cap your hole, but small enough to be manageable.

Have one person stand on a raised mound of snow inside the shelter, and someone else outside passing blocks up the side. With a snow saw, smooth the edge of the hole, angling it back at about 30 degrees. Once you have a smooth surface, move a block onto the edge long-wise. It should touch at the two ends. If necessary, carve out the middle of the bottom edge so that it is off the surface. The hardest part of this process is balancing the first block and bringing up the second. You can have someone on the outside helping. The blocks should lean in toward the center and touch at the top corner. Repeat the process until you have encircled the hole with snow blocks. If you have enough lean and a small enough hole, it may only take three blocks. Once you've made the cap, cut a block to fit into the hole left in the top and slide it into

Moling out a quinzhee can go faster if you have someone digging in from the door and from the top, but then you are left with a hole in your roof. You can close the hole with a cap made from blocks of snow. DON SHARAF

place. Now use small blocks of snow to fill in the gaps between the blocks.

SNOW KITCHENS

Snow allows you to create a comfortable place to cook, hang out, and store your gear. You can have benches and counters, shelves and cubbies. Often the best place to start is in the mounds of snow coming out of your snow shelter. If you aren't making a snow shelter, pile up snow and let it sit to work harden.

For a good basic kitchen, use a horseshoe shape. Make your counters about waist high, with a wall of

snow at the back to serve as a wind block. Kick in the bottom of the counter to give yourself space for your toes. You'll want to designate an area of clean snow where you'll collect snow for water. You'll also want to make a sump hole for wastewater. All food scraps should be strained out of the water and packed out. Make sure the two areas are well-known, so you don't mix them.

Carve out benches for sitting and cubbies to store your gear. You'll also need a water storage spot. Dig into the bottom of the counter, creating a space large enough for a pot. At the end of the evening, before you go to bed, you can put a pot full of water into the storage space, block it off with food bags or a backpack, and the water will remain unfrozen overnight.

You can build a fully enclosed kitchen quinzhee, an outdoor kitchen with snow walls, or even create a kitchen inside a tarp, depending on your time and energy. Indoor kitchens make cooking warm and cozy when storms roll in, but you need to make sure they are vented adequately to avoid carbon monoxide poisoning.

SARAH CARPENTER

A nice winter kitchen is protected from the wind, has counters and cubbies for working and storage, and benches to sit on. ALLEN O'BANNON

ORGANIZATION

Life in the winter is much easier if you are organized and efficient. Develop a system for dealing with your equipment and sharing chores. If you are disorganized, you are likely to lose things and be uncomfortable. In the kitchen, make sure you consolidate your belongings before you go to bed. It is nice to have a spice rack while you are preparing a meal, but if you leave all your spices lined up on the counter and it dumps snow overnight, you are unlikely to find your salt again.

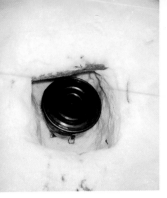

It's nice to go to bed with at least one pot of water ready for the morning. To store the water overnight so that it doesn't freeze, make a pit in the snow, place the pot on a pad inside the pit, and cover with either a food bag or a snow block. ALLEN O'BANNON

Close up your kitchen at night or when you leave camp for the day. Put all your food into a zip bag or backpack or in a single cubby on your counter. Fill your fuel bottles, so the next person in the kitchen can start cooking right away.

Make sure you have plenty of liquid water on hand before you put your stove away, the water bottles are full, and at least one pot is ready to go. That saves you time and energy, especially on cold, snowy mornings.

Stick your skis or snowshoes up in the snow, so they are easy to see. Hang your poles off of them rather than sticking them into the snow where they can get frozen in place. If you have a sled, flip it over and lean it up against a tree or the wall of your snow kitchen, so it doesn't fill up with snow or get buried in a dump.

GOING TO BED

Getting into bed can be a bit of an ordeal, as it requires lots of changing, fluffing, and moving around to make yourself comfortable. In the tight space of a confined snow shelter, it's often a good idea for one person at a time to go in and get ready for bed. That prevents a lot of elbowing and bumping and lost gear. Your tent mates can be closing down the kitchen while you are getting ready.

Make sure you are warm before you get into bed. Think of your body as a furnace; it needs to be turned on and generating heat if you want to stay comfortable. So eat a good dinner to give you lots of fuel. If you have chilled down while hanging out around the kitchen, consider a quick jog or ski around camp to get your muscles moving. Do some jumping jacks; anything to pump the blood around and chase off the chill. This is also a good time for one last pee before you hunker down for the night. Once you feel comfortable, head into your shelter.

Before you move into the sleeping chamber, brush all the snow off your body. The temperature inside will be quite warm and the snow will melt, making things wet, so it's important to get it off outside. You may consider carrying a brush to do this.

When you are snow-free, you can crawl inside and make your bed. Spread out your sleeping pads, making sure the half-pad is under your torso. You can then remove your big insulating outwear and lay it down on top of your pad for extra cushioning and insulation from the ground. You can also wrap your parka around your feet if you tend to get cold in your extremities. A hot-water bottle (with the lid securely closed) inside your sleeping bag down by your feet can be heavenly.

What you sleep in is determined by personal preference. Most people seem to be comfortable sleeping in their base layers, a dry pair of socks, and a hat. If it's really cold, you can add a pile sweater or a neck warmer. If it's really, really cold (unlikely in a snow shelter, but possible in a tent), don't hesitate to put on your insulated parka and pants, just make sure you aren't too cramped in your bag.

Sleep with damp clothes—socks, boot liners, gloves—to help them dry and keep them from freezing. Some warm-bodied people can toss these items in their sleeping bag and wake up to find the clothes warm and dry. Others may find the moisture prevents them from sleeping well. If that's the case with you, you can put your damp gear between your two sleeping pads. It won't dry in this location, but it won't freeze either. You can always take advantage of the sun or wear the items on your body during the day to do the rest of the job. Or if you are sleeping with a hot-water bottle, put your damp gear near it to help the gear dry.

Some people like to sleep with a snack close by in case they get cold or hungry during the night. You can make a little cubby in the wall of your shelter to store your snack, headlamp, pee bottle, and any other items you might need during the night. ***Note:*** In general winter campers do not need to be overly concerned about hibernating bears, but bears can be active in the fall and early spring. Check with land managers in the area to find out if there has been any bear activity reported. Keep an eye out for bear tracks. If you see bear sign, it's time to store your food away from your sleeping area.

You should know that it is likely you will wake up at least once. Winter nights are long and mean lots of hours lying prone in your bag. You can bring cards, portable games (some people draw backgammon or chess boards on their sleeping pads), or a book to entertain you so you don't have to try to sleep for too long, but even then if the sun is setting before 6 p.m. and rising after 8 a.m., you'll probably be in your bag for ten hours a night on average. Inevitably, you'll need to pee, adjust your layers, or shift your body. Don't fight it. The urge to pee will not go away. Get up and go out or use your bottle. You'll still have plenty of time to sleep. If you get cold, do some sit-ups in your bag or have a snack. Relax and don't fret about being awake.

GETTING UP IN THE MORNING

Again, it's easiest to have one person getting up at a time if you are in a confined space. You may want to designate who is on for breakfast the night before, so he or she gets up first.

Your bag may be damp in morning. There's lots of moisture coming off your body and from the wet

Tips for Comfort

» Insulate everything. Everything left out freezes in the winter, so make sure you insulate things you don't want frozen: water bottles, contact lens solution, candy bars.

» Start with a small hot-water bottle at the beginning of the day. A hot bottle makes a great hand warmer, plus it takes much longer to cool down to freezing.

» Wear your damp clothes until they dry. Drape socks over your shoulders or tuck them into the waistband of your long underwear.

» Avoid getting overly sweaty by changing clothing to allow cooling.

» Sleep with your boot liners or boots to keep them from freezing. Today's thermal liners don't absorb much water, so you can get away with not actually bringing them into your sleeping bag with you. But unfrozen doesn't mean warm. If you tend to have cold feet, sleeping with your liners will help minimize the shock of putting on your boots on a frosty morning. If you have plenty of fuel, make a hot-water bottle and stick it into your liners to warm them up before putting them on.

» If you anticipate really cold temperatures, bring a few chemical hand and toe warmers to stick in your pocket, mitten, or boot. They can be a nice luxury.

clothes you slept with, so it's a good idea to bring your bag out of the shelter to air it. Stick your skis in the snow and hang your bag between them with the zipper open. If the sun is out, the bag will dry quickly. If it's not, the moisture will still evaporate, especially in a breeze. This works even if it is snowing, as long as the snow is not too wet. You'll know the difference: If snow is melting on your jacket, it's too wet to air your bag. If it can be brushed off without leaving a damp spot, evaporation will still work.

USING THE BATHROOM

Peeing in the winter is easy. If you have to go, you go. Around camp it's a good idea to designate a urinal of sorts. This ensures you don't inadvertently contaminate your water supply.

Pooping is a different matter. In most of parts of the country, you'll find it impossible to dig a cat hole in the dirt in the winter, which means the traditional way of disposing of your waste can't be used. The best technique in lieu of a cat hole is to pack your waste out. There are a number of products on the market designed to allow you to pack out your poop—WAG bags, Restop, and the like. These bags allow you to dispose of your waste in a regular trashcan after a trip.

If you are out for an extended trip, it can be hard to pack out all your waste. So in the absence of dirt

Human Waste Disposal

As more people venture into the wilderness, there are an increasing number of areas with regulations dictating the proper way to dispose of human waste. You may be required to pack it out. Be sure to check with the land management agency in charge of the area you plan to visit to find out if it has guidelines in place for human waste disposal. In the absence of specific regulations, follow the techniques outlined in this chapter.

or the feasibility of a WAG bag (and as long as there are no regulations to the contrary), you are left with burying your waste in the snow.

Give yourself a little time to do your business. You'll want to put on your skis or snowshoes, so you can get away from water, camp, or the trail. Two hundred feet is a good distance. If you don't know what that looks like, think about your pacing. Most of us average 3 to 4 foot pacing, so you are going to move about 70 paces away before you drop your drawers.

Obviously water is frozen in the winter in most places, but you still want to be away from lakeshores or drainages, because once the snow melts your feces will be exposed and can get into the water source.

Stomp out an area in the snow. You may then want to remove your skis or snowshoes, depending on your stability and ability to spread your legs wide enough to ensure a clean deposit. No one wants "brown klister" on his or her skis. Punch a hole in the middle of your platform with your ski pole, and you are good to go.

Ideal poop spots are located near trees, where the snow is shallower and you can grab on to something to provide stability.

Your choice of toilet paper includes natural TP (like snow) or paper. You can mold a snowball into a body-conforming shape if you have the right type of snow. The advantage of snow is that it cleans as it wipes, which is nice in the winter when bathing is impossible. But snow is cold and can be uncomfortable, so you may want to bring some TP. You'll just have to pack it out with you, which is not big deal if you double bag it in plastic.

After you finish, cover your deposit with snow. You don't have to bury it too deeply. In fact, the warmth of the sun is critical to the eventual decomposition of your feces, but you also don't want your teammates or others following behind you to accidentally encounter your poop.

Now wash your hands. Poor hygiene is a leading cause of illness in the backcountry. So make sure you get your hands clean. You can do this by rubbing snow vigorously in your hands to wash them and use hand sanitizer for a final cleanse.

COOKING

Planning Your Menu

To come up with a meal plan for your trip, think lots of food, lots of calories, not much prep. Simple one-pot meals are preferable to elaborate concoctions that take lots of time, fuel, and preparation to make, so things like mac and cheese, beans and rice with cheese, cheesy potatoes, chili with cheese, curried rice, and the like work well. Note the emphasis on cheese. Cheese is a great source of calories and fat in the winter, so it's not a bad idea to throw it in just about everything you eat. But some people don't like or can't eat cheese. If that's you, consider other options that will give you the calories and fat you need. These include meat, butter, and nut butters.

In general, make sure your ration contains roughly twice as many calories as you'd carry in the summer. You need the extra fuel to stay warm and energized.

You can bring frozen food—veggies, meat, even pizza—in the winter, which is a nice treat. Frozen food is heavy, so this option is really best suited for long trips when you are pulling a sled and weight is of less concern.

Prepping Food in Town

On the plus side, winter temperatures allow food to keep indefinitely. On the downside, it's hard to work with a big chunk of frozen food. It's a good idea to

The more organized and efficient you are in the winter, the easier your life will be. Tips for comfortable winter living include: insulate everything from the cold, place hot items on pads to keep them from melting into the snow, wear wool gloves while cooking so you can handle hot items, and build a counter so you can prepare meals while standing. ALLEN O'BANNON

chop your food—cheese, butter, meat, chocolate—into bite-sized pieces before you leave the warmth of your home.

Cooking Tips

Winter camping is all about tricks. Knowing the little things can make your life a whole lot easier. For example, if you leave your lighter in your stove bag, like many of us do in the summer, it will get damp and cold and will not work. So carry lighters in small plastic bags and stash them in your pockets—usually a few different pockets—so you always have one handy.

Another trick is to cover your stove with a pot overnight. This keeps it from filling up with snow, but also allows you to leave it out, so you don't have to reassemble it in the cold of the morning.

Wear lightweight wool gloves around the kitchen, especially when filling the stove. Gas can become supercooled in the winter, causing superficial frostbite if it comes into contact with your skin. Wool gloves, rather than polypropylene gloves, are best because you can use them as potholders where synthetic gloves would melt.

STOVE USE

Lighting stoves in the cold can be challenging, so you need to baby them a bit. That means keeping them out of the snow and allowing them to prime for an adequate length of time. Assuming you are using a white gas stove like MSR's Whisperlite, if temperatures drop below zero, you should actually pour fuel (rather than pumping up the stove and opening the on valve to allow liquid fuel to escape) into the spirit cup. Fill the cup to the brim and light the fuel. This is probably more fuel than you normally use to prime your stove, and you'll have a bit of a campfire going for a few seconds, so choose your location wisely. But it's worth allowing your stove plenty of time to get warm, so the liquid fuel will vaporize and burn efficiently.

Make sure you are ready to use the stove before you turn it on, as it's a pain and a waste of gas to constantly light it and turn it off. So be ready and keep the stove burning until your meal is done and

White gas stoves work best in low temperatures so are the most reliable stove for winter use. Make sure to use plenty of liquid fuel to prime your stove so that it works regardless of how cold it is outside. MOLLY ABSOLON

you've got plenty of water. Other ways to maximize your stove's performance are to use a windscreen and to build a protected alcove for your stove in the snow. Always use a lid when you are cooking, so heat doesn't escape.

CLEANUP

The other advantage to simple one-pot meals is to minimize cleanup. You don't have to worry a ton about dirty dishes in the winter in terms of germs, but it's nice to have clean pots and pans for your next meal. Warm up some water and use it to get food residue off the sides of your dishes. Strain the wastewater as you pour it out, bagging up any food scraps to be packed out. Rinse the dish with a bit more warm water, and you are done.

Chapter Four

Winter Travel: Choosing a Mode of Transportation

SNOWSHOES

Humans figured out how to move over the top of the snow thousands of years ago, when they first moved into snowy climates. It was either that or die, to be blunt, because human feet are too small and our weight too concentrated to be able to move on top of most snow conditions. We just punch in and wallow, unable to cover any ground and wasting precious energy needed to survive. Our ancestors created snowshoes and skis, so they could stay on top of the snow. Snowshoes copy the same adaptation seen in many winter animals: oversized feet.

Snowshoes represent a relatively inexpensive, easy way to break into winter travel. There are many styles of snowshoes made for everything from cross-country running to mountaineering, with plenty of options in between for those of us who prefer a simple stroll through the woods.

You can spend as little as $100 or as much as $300 or more on a pair of snowshoes. A great place to start figuring out what is best for you is the online website Backpacker.com/gear where you can search for snowshoes or snowshoeing tips.

Snowshoes come in a variety of styles and sizes, designed for different uses and snow conditions. In general, the bigger the snowshoe, the better it is in deep powder away from packed trails. MOLLY ABSOLON

Fitness snowshoes tend to be smaller and lighter than other models, so you can run over packed or groomed trails. They do not have a lot of flotation, so if you venture off firm snow, you are likely to sink down or posthole. Often fitness snowshoes have a fixed binding, which means the tail is attached to the binding with an elastic strap that keeps it from dragging along behind you. This feature is great for running, but is less ideal for moving up and down a slope where you want more ankle flexibility.

Recreational snowshoes are all-around snowshoes and are best for beginners or those who are looking for a way to get outside and explore their local park, but don't have any interest in venturing too far afield. Recreational snowshoes tend to be the least expensive option available, so the materials may not be quite as durable as more heavy-duty models. The bindings on these snowshoes are less aggressive than other models, so they don't perform as well in steep terrain. They also tend to be small, which means they are not good for people who plan to carry a lot of heavy gear. But they are ideal for the casual user in easy to moderate terrain and hiking on packed trails in rolling hills.

The next step up is a **hiking snowshoe** that is just a little beefier and bigger than the recreational models. Hiking snowshoes are better suited for off-trail travel and are usually equipped with cleats under foot to allow you to kick your way up steep slopes, making them suitable for the majority of winter hiking uses. These models may have a climbing bar attached to the binding to support your heel on uphills.

Backcountry or mountaineering snowshoes are designed to tackle steep terrain and support heavy loads. They offer the most flotation under foot of any model to accommodate the combined weight of a person and gear. They have the beefiest bindings, with climbing bars to use under your heel on steep ascents. The cleats have aggressive prongs to bite into firm snow. The bindings are made to hold bigger boots (snowboard or mountaineering boots), and the snowshoes are made from stronger materials to ensure durability. These snowshoes are big, tough, and expensive, and for many of us they are overkill. Think about what you plan to do, talk

Almost anyone who can walk can snowshoe, making this a great way to explore winter for all ages. ERIC MICHAUD, THINKSTOCK

to an expert, and choose accordingly. You can often rent snowshoes to try them out before you make a purchase.

To help you narrow down the options further, ask yourself the following questions:

» What do you weigh and how much gear do you intend to carry? The heavier that combined weight, the bigger the size of the snowshoes you will need.

» What snow conditions do you expect to encounter? Dry powdery snow requires a bigger snowshoe than firm, wet snow or packed trails.

Boots

For most snowshoeing, you will want to wear hiking boots to provide support and insulation so your feet stay warm. Some snowshoes are designed to be worn with mountaineering boots, but that isn't necessary for more lightweight, recreational models. Often a pack boot or light-hiking boot is adequate. Make sure your boots have plenty of space for warm socks, room to wiggle your toes, some insulation for warmth, and enough integrity to support the snowshoe's binding straps without cutting into your ankle and foot.

Snowshoes work with most winter boots, as long as they have enough integrity to support the binding. WANDERLUSTER, THINKSTOCK

Poles

If you are just walking around the golf course on your snowshoes, you won't need poles, but once you get off the beaten track and into powdery snow, poles can be a great asset for balance, impulsion, and support. You can use a pair of trekking poles (change out the basket for a bigger snow basket so that the pole doesn't plunge down through the snow to the ground) or regular ski poles. The advantage of trekking poles is that you can shorten or lengthen them for going up and down hills.

People say if you can walk, you can snowshoe, and this is essentially true, especially if you stick to easy terrain and packed trails. But there are some movements that can be tricky, such as walking along a side hill. Here are a few tricks that can help you adapt to walking around with large platters attached to your feet.

Level Ground

On level ground you really don't need much coaching, but it helps to think about walking with a slightly wider stance than normal, so you don't accidentally trip yourself up by stepping on the opposite snowshoe as

Lifting your knees higher than normal helps your snowshoe clear the snow. THINKSTOCK

you move forward. In general, try to maintain an easy, natural gait. In deeper snow, exaggerate your knee lift to help your snowshoe clear the snow.

Uphill

The easiest way to walk uphill in snowshoes is to go straight up instead of switching back and forth across the slope. The bindings on snowshoes pivot, allowing you to kick your toes into the snow to form a step as you move upward. Most snowshoes have a cleat beneath your foot that will give you purchase in slippery conditions. Try not to lean forward. Rather, stand upright with your weight centered on the ball of your foot. This position gives you the best traction as you climb.

In snowshoes, it's easiest to travel straight uphill, kicking your toes into the snow to make a step. JUPITERIMAGES, THINKSTOCK

If you decide to cross the slope diagonally, stomp down with your snowshoe to create a level platform for your foot. Snowshoes do not really allow you to flex your ankle side to side effectively, so you'll need to transform the side hill into a flat path to be able to traverse it comfortably. In firm snow, side hilling becomes increasingly difficult.

Downhill

Again, because of the geometry of the snowshoe, you are best heading straight down a slope rather than trying to traverse. Face downhill and bend at your hips so your "nose is over your toes." This position keeps your weight centered over your feet. If you lean back, you are likely to fall on your butt and slide down the slope, which could actually be fun and fast, but if you prefer to walk, use this body position.

Plunge your heel down into the snow. Be aggressive so your heel sinks in, leaving you with a solid platform to stand on. Lift your knees high to move the snowshoe forward.

In firm snow, this can be difficult. If you cannot get your heels into the snow, you may need to find another way down.

Consider the runout if you think you could fall. If the slope ends in rocks or water, make sure you can stop yourself in case you slip.

Breaking Trail

If you are on a packed trail, it doesn't matter who goes out front, but if you choose to branch off and travel in untracked snow, the person in front is going to be working a lot harder than those following behind. It helps to switch leaders frequently to share the load and conserve your energy. Those of you in the back can step in the leader's footsteps and have an easier time. If you want to pack down the track even more, you can step half-in, half-out of the prints to create a bigger platform of compressed snow for the people in back. This technique breaks down the snow walls between the footprints and gradually creates one continuous track that makes for easy traveling.

Falling Down and Getting Up

It's not uncommon for people to get tangled up in their snowshoes and end up toppling over. Fortunately, snow is soft, and falls are usually more amusing than they are dangerous. If you lose your balance, try not to stick out a hand to save yourself as you can dislocate your shoulder or hurt your wrist if you come down hard on the extended limb. Your best bet is to sit down on your butt or to tuck your shoulder and roll so you take the brunt of the impact in your upper back.

Once you are on the ground, you'll find it can be hard to stand back up without anything to push off

It's not uncommon to get tangled up in your snowshoes and fall down, especially with a playful dog in the way. JENNY CHARLES

of. If you are using ski poles, you can make an X with them on the snow and press down at the central point of intersection. Push yourself forward onto your knees and then stand up. Without poles, you can use your pack as a platform or grab onto a tree or shrub to give yourself something firm to pull on.

CROSS-COUNTRY SKIING

Skis

Skis come in all shapes and sizes. You can spend a lot of money on your setup or very little if you shop around and look for used gear. You can find skis designed for travel on groomed tracks or ones intended purely for powder skiing. You will need to do a little research to figure out what type of ski is best suited for your goals. The best place to start is at a ski

To determine what type of ski is appropriate, consider what you want to do and where you want to go. Lightweight Nordic skis like this woman is using are best for touring on groomed trails. MOLLY ABSOLON

shop. Most stores will have knowledgeable staff who can guide you to the right equipment based on your specific desires. Tell the staff person exactly what you hope to do and what kind of skier you are, so he or she can help you narrow down your options.

Magazines and online forums can be helpful if you want to compare brands and styles. Most ski magazines do yearly gear reviews that can help you sort through the marketing hype. Friends can also be a great source of information.

Finally, many ski towns will have consignment stores or annual ski swaps where you can buy used gear. If you are just starting out in the sport, this is a great place to begin. It helps to go shopping with someone who can help you sort through the junk, but with a little perseverance and a willingness to dig, you may find some great deals.

Cross-country skiing comes in a variety of styles. The common denominator that sets it apart from downhill skiing is that you can free your heel, so it can move up and down. This freedom allows you to walk on your skis. Aside from that general commonality, cross-country skiing styles can be pretty different, depending on the type of skis you wear.

Your options include:

» Skate skis—limited to groomed tracks
» Classic cross-country skis, in different weights and widths for different conditions
» Backcountry touring skis—usually have some camber plus metal edges for control on descents. Camber refers to the slight arch of your skis.
» Downhill backcountry skis: just what they sound like: skis made primarily for descending. You can tour in these skis, but often they are clunky and slow. They usually don't have much camber (or may have reverse camber), which makes them hard to kick and glide on, and

The primary difference between touring skis and backcountry downhill skis is their camber. Touring skis have double camber, which allows you to rise off the surface of the snow for gliding. Backcountry touring skis have single camber, designed for contact with the snow for turning. MOLLY ABSOLON

they always have metal edges and a beefier binding designed for turning. These are the skis you want if you plan to tour up hills to ski down.

To determine which of these models is best suited for your goals, ask yourself the following questions:

» Do I want to tour or make turns?
» Do I want to stick to groomed trails or venture off trail?

For groomed track skiing, you have two options: skate skis or lightweight classic skis. Lightweight classic skis are better for exploring in winter. Skate skis are more about moving fast.

For off-trail cross-country skiing, you will want to find a double-camber touring ski that's a little bit

Lightweight cross-country touring skis are perfect for packed trails and novice skiers and are a good way to get people of all ages out and about in the winter. MOLLY ABSOLON

wider than the lightweight gear used for set tracks. When unweighted, this bow rises up off the ground allowing you to glide forward. When weighted, the skis flattens out and the kick wax or fish scales that provide traction comes into contact with the snow, allowing you to propel yourself forward.

If you plan to go on extended off-trail tours on your skis, you might want to consider a pair with metal edges. This adds weight to your setup and will slow down your kick and glide, but the edges give you control on descents, which can be a lifesaver if your route involves icy, tight trails through the woods (think New England).

For backcountry downhill skiing, you'll want a single camber, metal-edged ski. Backcountry or alpine touring is exploding in popularity, and there are many skis out there to choose from. Things to consider include the typical snow conditions you'll encounter, your style of skiing, and your weight and height. You'll also need to choose between an alpine touring binding that allows you to lock your heel down on the descent or a telemark binding, where your heel remains free and you make turns by dropping one knee. Alpine touring is easier, but many people prefer the challenge and beauty of the telemark turn.

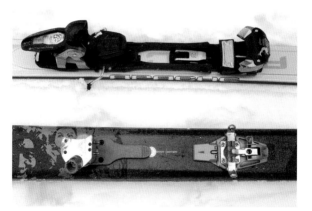

Different styles of alpine touring bindings allow you to free your heel for travel and then lock it down for descents. The lighter-weight models are best if you plan to spend most of your time out of bounds. Heavyweight alpine touring bindings are good for skiers who only venture out into the backcountry from a ski resort. MOLLY ABSOLON

Boots

Your boots will be determined by the type of skiing you choose to do. The one thing to keep in mind if you plan to go winter camping on your skis is warmth and comfort. Lightweight backcountry ski boots tend to be a bit more useful on multiday trips. You can use a beefier, performance downhill boot, but you may be uncomfortable on long tours, and if they fit tightly, your feet could be prone to cold.

Downhill ski boots have a plastic shell with removable liners that you can sleep with at night to keep warm. Lightweight cross-country touring boots usually don't have this option, which makes them a little cold for overnight trips. You'll probably want to sleep with them to keep them from freezing if you head out in classic cross-country ski boots. Make sure your boots are roomy enough for thick socks, so you'll stay warm in cold conditions.

Poles

There are a surprising number of options for ski poles. Usually, the type you use will be dictated primarily by your choice of ski, but even then, you'll be forced to make some decisions. Nordic poles are long and come with small baskets. They range in price from less than $100 up to around $300. The pricier poles are lightweight and designed for racing, so for the most part, you won't need to make that kind of expenditure. If you plan to be off packed trails, look

The type of pole you use in the winter is dictated by the type of skiing you plan to do. Long poles with small baskets are designed for Nordic skiing on groomed trails. Telescoping poles with big baskets are good for backcountry ski touring, as they can be lengthened for travel and shortened for descents. MOLLY ABSOLON

at the basket on your poles. A lot of cross-country ski poles have wimpy baskets that will plunge down through the snow if it isn't packed down. So for off-trail travel, your best bet is to switch to a larger basket that is designed to stay on the surface.

For downhill backcountry skiing, you can use regular alpine ski poles with a big basket, or you may opt for telescoping poles, so you can lengthen them for touring when you want lots of reach, but can then shorten them for skiing downhill.

Wax or No Wax

Historically, waxless skis were slow and a little clunky, but the technology has improved, and today waxless skis with fish scales or ridges underfoot to provide traction are popular and effective. For many people, wax is becoming obsolete. But some people like to

Fish scales or ridges in the base of your skis provide traction for kicking and mean you don't need to worry about which wax to use on any given day. MOLLY ABSOLON

use wax. If you get wax right, you'll enjoy more glide. If you get it wrong, you may find yourself cursing your choice.

There are two kinds of wax: glide and kick wax. Glide wax is the kind you use to coat the bottom of your skis. It helps keep the bases from drying out and allows you to move more smoothly over the snow. Kick wax is the kind you get in little metal canisters that you rub on to the bottom of your ski, in what is known as the wax pocket. Kick wax sticks to the snow, providing traction so you can move forward on the flats or up slight hills.

If you opt to use kick wax, you'll find you have many choices, all color-coded according to the temperature of the snow. In general, the warmer the color, the warmer the snow. Don't overthink it. Waxing can be a science project and, if you are racing, that project can be the difference between winning and losing. But if you plan to tour around in the trees, and especially if you are on big, clunky skis, you can afford to be a little less picky. If you have a long, flat approach to navigate en route to the slopes, you may find kick wax useful even on your big downhill backcountry skis. Some people opt to put on their skins for these kinds of approaches, but you'll move faster using wax.

To determine your wax color, pick up a clump of snow. If it makes a wet snowball, use red wax. If it's a dry snowball, try something in the purple range, moving down into blue. Blue wax is colder, so if your snowball isn't holding together quite as well, use blue. Finally, if the snow just falls through your fingers, look at a green wax. You can also opt to use a two-wax system—wet and dry—if you want to simplify things even further.

Err on the cold side when you put your first coat of wax on your skis. You can think of wax like making a peanut butter and jelly sandwich. You can't spread peanut butter on top of jelly. Likewise, it's hard to spread a hard, cold wax on top of a gooey warm one.

Finally, don't be afraid to put the wax on thickly. You can smooth it out with a cork if you want, but if you're traveling off trail through fresh snow, the wax wears off quickly and usually too much isn't an issue.

Carry a plastic or metal scraper in your pocket, so you can remove excess wax or ice and snow buildup if necessary.

Skins

Most backcountry downhill skiers use climbing skins, rather than wax or fish scales, on the bottom of their skis to grip the snow. Climbing skins provide more purchase on the uphill, but they are slow on the flats, so are best suited for ascending.

Originally made from animal fur, climbing skins are configured so that they are smooth in one direction and rough in the other. Fibers on the skins catch on the snow and keep you from sliding backward

Skin Emergency

At some point you may experience skin failure. Halfway up a slope, your skin slips off, refusing to stick to the bottom of your ski any longer. If you find yourself in this predicament, take your ski off and prop it up in the snow, then take your skin and wrap it around the ski, glue side in. Run the skin rapidly back and forth to scrape off any snow or ice that has built up on the glue. You can also run the skin across your thigh if you prefer. Your goal is to warm up the surface of the skin and give the glue a bit more life. Duct tape or ski straps can also be used to help secure the skin to your ski if all else fails.

In wet snow conditions, skins absorb water and can ice up. A wax is available to coat the bottom of your skis and prevent snow buildup. Carrying this so-called gob stopper is advisable in the spring, when the snow is wet. If you find yourself with snow build-up and no wax, scrape off the snow and apply sunscreen to the skin. Sometimes this helps prevent snow buildup.

To store skins between use, fold them together, sticky sides in.
MOLLY ABSOLON

downhill. Today, most climbing skins are made from mohair or nylon and are coated with a sticky glue that adheres to the base of your ski. A tip and tail attachment is usually used to hold the skins in place.

Store skins by folding them together with the glue side facing in. The skins will stick together and stay cleaner this way. Too much dirt and lint in the glue will make the skins less sticky.

To put the skins on, pull them apart (which can be hard with new skins, so you may want to have someone help you). Place the tip clasp over the tip, and smooth the skin down along the base of the ski, making sure it doesn't stick out on the sides. Attach the tail clasp, and you're set.

At the top of your climb, strip the skins off, fold them up, and store them inside your backpack or in a pocket. Avoid dropping your skins in the snow, as it will affect the glue's adhesive power. If you are camping, hang your skins out to dry while you make camp. When you go to bed, bring your skins into your shelter with you. You can place them between your sleeping bag and pad to keep them from freezing and to help with drying.

Travel Techniques

Flats

On flat or rolling terrain, you propel yourself forward by a technique called kick and glide. It's not a hard technique to learn—although perfecting it can take lots of practice. But for touring around in the woods, you don't have to worry about perfection.

Stand with your knees bent, ankles flexed, and feet shoulder-width apart. This athletic stance is your basic position. You'll want to hold these angles in your ankles and knees throughout the movement. Slide one foot forward, keeping your ankle flexed and your knee over your toes. This is important. The classic beginner error is to shoot that foot too far forward, so your toe is pointing out, which makes it hard to move onto that foot. Shift all your weight over to your forward foot, pushing your rear foot back and straight. This backward push is the kick. Hold or glide

The kick and glide technique is used to travel over flat or rolling terrain. It's a natural kind of exaggerated shuffle across the snow. MOLLY ABSOLON

The classic beginner error is to be too stiff and straight-legged. Remember to stay in an athletic stance with your knees bent and ankles flexed. MOLLY ABSOLON

in this position until you feel yourself slowing down, then bring your rear leg forward, shift your weight onto that ski and push back with the other. It's really just an exaggerated jogging motion, and most likely, you'll find the movement comes pretty easily. It may take a while to gain your balance, however, so start with small strides.

Your arms will swing naturally in opposition with your legs, just like running. That means when your right leg is forward, your right arm is back, and vice versa.

Bend your forward arm, planting the pole beside your toe. You'll then push into that hand, straightening your arm as you move past the pole. This pole plant adds to your forward momentum.

Uphill Technique

For low angle hills, you can just shorten your stride, increase your cadence, and shuffle up the incline. Take care not to lean forward as you climb. You need to weight your wax or the fish scales to maintain purchase, so try to keep your weight centered over your feet.

At some point, the slope will become too steep to allow you to continue to kick and glide up it. This angle is dictated by your technique and whether you are using skins or wax. Skins can climb a lot steeper than wax. But all uphill techniques have their limits. When you reach yours, you have a few options:

Switchbacks: The most energy-efficient technique will be to cut across the slope, weaving your

For low angle ascents, just shorten your kick and glide stride and keep your body erect. If you lean too far forward, you will slip backward. MOLLY ABSOLON

way back and forth upward. This way you can minimize the angle of your climb.

Herringbone: The herringbone is made by creating a V with your skis, open-side facing up the hill. Roll your ankles in slightly, so your skis are up on their edge, and step uphill, one foot after the other. The herringbone works well on steep slopes, but it is tiring and slow, so it is best used for short stretches.

Side step: To side step, stand across the slope with your ankles turned slightly into the hill. This allows that uphill edge to dig into the snow. Step your high foot up hill, then follow with your downhill foot, gradually stepping sideways upward. Side stepping is

When the slope is too steep to shuffle your way to the top, make a V-shape with your skis, roll your ankles in to set the inside edge, and herringbone your way up. MOLLY ABSOLON

useful for climbing out of a creek bottom or alongside hills, but it can be a little tricky when your heel is free and the tail of your ski drags. If you are wearing AT gear (Alpine Touring gear), you may want to lock your heel down if you anticipate side stepping for a long distance. The key to this technique is to keep your skis perpendicular to the fall line to prevent slipping.

Kick Turns

The easiest way to turn around on skis is to simply walk around in a kind of star shape. But sometimes you can't do that, especially if you are making switchbacks up a relatively steep slope. Here you'll have to do a kick turn. Kick turns can be a little balancey, so it's worth practicing them on level ground before you tackle one on a slope.

Position your skis across the fall line. Stomp out a stable platform. Lift your uphill ski, keeping the tip high. Arc the ski around so that its tip is facing the same direction as the tail of your other ski. Place that ski on the snow and stomp down to make sure it is secure. Transfer your weight onto the uphill ski and swing the downhill ski up and around, ending with it on the uphill side of the ski you are standing on.

Going Downhill

This book is not about teaching you to make an alpine or telemark turn. But for general touring, you do need to know how to go downhill, even when you are just looping around a golf course. For low angle downhills in powdery snow, you can let your skis glide in a parallel position, making what people call "elevensies." But if conditions are icy or steep, or you have to make a turn, this technique quickly gets you going too fast to make any quick changes in direction, especially if you are wearing lightweight, edgeless skis.

To control your speed on descents, make a wedge shape with your skis and roll your ankles in to set an edge to create what is called a snowplow. MOLLY ABSOLON

The best technique for these conditions is a snowplow or wedge. You do it just like it sounds: put your skis into a V-shape with the open end facing uphill, roll your ankles in to set your edge and off you go. You'll notice it's just the opposite of the herringbone and is pretty darn effective for slowing you down. Some people put their poles between their legs and weight them by sitting down on them (don't put all your weight on the poles or they will break). Your poles act as a kind of brake as you careen downhill.

Finally, use the terrain to help control your descent. You can dump a lot of speed by moving into untracked powder or by picking the lowest angle line down the slope.

Breaking Trail

In deep snow, breaking trail is hard, so it's best to take turns being out in front. Look ahead and plan your route as you move up, so you don't walk yourself into a roadblock. Look for low angle slopes, ridges, or open woods without a lot of shrubbery to negotiate. Try to make rounded turns to minimize the number of kick turns you have to make.

Falling Down and Getting Up

Falling is inevitable on skis. You may fall because you are just learning how to ski. You may fall to stop

Getting up after a fall in deep powder can be awkward and strenuous. Try to get your skis downhill and across the fall line and consider taking off your pack to make it easier to move.

MOLLY ABSOLON

Getting up from a fall in soft snow can be awkward and tiring. Your best bet is to get your skis parallel to each other and then roll forward onto your knee using your poles placed as an X on the surface of the snow to push off with. MOLLY ABSOLON

quickly. You may fall because the snow conditions are challenging and you lose your balance.

It can be hard to get up after falling. If you are wearing a pack, jettison it, as the weight can add to the awkwardness. Try to roll into a position where your skis are parallel and across the fall line. Make an X with your poles on the uphill side and push down on that with your hand to give you some leverage as you come to standing. Bend forward onto your knees first and then straighten up. If you get really tangled up in your fall, you may just want to take off your skis to get untangled and back on your feet.

OTHER MODES OF TRAVEL

There are a number of other ways to travel across the surface of the snow that you might want to consider. Splitboards, or snowboards that come apart and can be used like skis, are a great option for snowboarders who want to go into the backcountry. Most of the techniques used on a splitboard for travel are the same as for skis.

You may live in a place where traveling on foot is an option in the winter, either because you don't get much snow or there are packed trails that are easy to follow without snowshoes or skis. Be careful going too far on foot if you plan to be out for an extended period. If a storm rolls in and dumps a couple of feet of snow on the ground, you may find yourself in a challenging situation as travel will become slow and difficult in deep snow without some flotation under your feet. The miles you covered quickly on your way in could take days to retrace on your way out if you have to wallow through the snow.

Chapter Five

Winter Hazards

Winter's magic is not without its dangers. Weather, cold, avalanches, and open water can quickly turn a jaunt into the backcountry into a deadly epic. You can minimize your exposure to these hazards when you pick your destination. Respect your experience level, have some kind of communication device (a personal-locating beacon or cell phone) that allows you to contact help, carry the appropriate equipment to cope with an emergency, and bone up on the skills and knowledge needed to be comfortable out in the winter.

If you are a novice winter camper, stay close to roads, so you can get out quickly if things go wrong. You don't have to go far to enjoy the peace and quiet of the winter environment, which means you can still enjoy camping out in the snow without the commitment of being miles and miles from help.

WINTER WEATHER

Winter weather itself can be harsh and demanding. A storm can blow in quickly, leaving you lost in a white-out with no sense of up, down, east, or west. People liken this experience to being inside a ping-pong ball. It can be very disorienting.

Conditions can change quickly in the winter when a storm blows in. Travelers can get in trouble if they continue to move despite deteriorating conditions. When whiteouts occur and snow is filling in your tracks, it's often time to stop and make camp to wait out the storm. ALLEN O'BANNON

Winter travelers most often get into trouble when they push on despite the deteriorating conditions. You may be able to follow a compass bearing effectively in a whiteout, but don't count on following your nose. There are way too many stories of people, convinced they knew exactly where they were going, walking around in circles.

If a storm blows in and you find yourself in a whiteout, your best bet is to stop and hunker down until you have better visibility.

Storms also bring in snow and wind, both of which can make travel difficult. Again, unless you are confident in your surroundings (and that means you know where you are, not you think you know where you are), don't try to move in a storm. It's easy to get lost and exhausted, both of which make you more prone to serious consequences.

Ultimately, cold is the killer. Cold is an inherent part of winter, and most of the time, you just deal with it by wearing more clothes, eating more food, carrying more gear, and creating elaborate camps that protect you from the elements. Sometimes, however, you may get too cold. If that happens, it's important to know what to do to keep a bad situation from turning into a deadly one.

ENVIRONMENTAL HAZARDS

Hypothermia

Hypothermia is when your core temperature drops below its comfortable 98.6°F average. There is a long continuum of decline as your body reacts to its falling temperature. First, you lose your fine motor skills. You can't zip up your jacket, and your coordination may seem off. Gradually, these signs intensify and are accompanied by changes in your ability to think rationally or make good decisions. You may begin to shiver uncontrollably.

People call this stage the "umbles" because those affected typically stumble, bumble, mumble, and grumble. Ideally, you want to stop this progression as quickly as possible. Watch your teammates and look for signs of the umbles. Keep track of yourself. If you find the zipper on your coat is suddenly really hard to operate, ask yourself if you are getting too cold.

With mild hypothermia such as this, you can usually stop the progression by exercising. Put your skis or snowshoes on and go for a quick jaunt. Do some jumping jacks, and swing your arms and legs. Often, it only takes a couple of minutes of moving around to get your furnace going again. Pay attention to why you got cold. Maybe you need to eat or drink something warm to fuel your engine. Maybe you need to get out of damp clothes and seek shelter from the wind. Your chill is a sign that you aren't dealing well with your environment. Stop and fix the problem before it gets worse.

As hypothermia progresses, people become increasingly apathetic. You may find you just want to sit down and do nothing. You may find talking difficult and be slow to respond to questions, or your responses may be inappropriate. As you get colder, your coordination continues to deteriorate, and you may be unable to walk without falling. Finally, a severely hypothermic person is catatonic. You may be unable to find his or her pulse. These people are in danger and are extremely fragile. They need to be rewarmed in a hospital.

For people who are moderately cold, start by making sure their clothes are dry and they are protected from the elements. If they are cogent and can drink without assistance, give them warm fluids and a snack. If these interventions produce no results, you may need to be more aggressive in your treatment. One of the most effective methods for treating moderate hypothermia is to make a hypothermia wrap (see sidebar).

If your patient is unresponsive, gently place her in a hypothermic wrap to prevent further heat loss and go for help. This person needs medical attention, but even if she appears dead, there is hope. Many severely hypothermic people have been successfully rewarmed at a hospital. First responders say, "Someone is never dead from the cold until they are warm and dead."

Frostbite

Frostbite occurs when tissue freezes, and it usually occurs on fingers, toes, or exposed parts of the face.

Frostbite is categorized like a burn. Its severity depends on the depth of the freezing in the skin: superficial, partial thickness, and full thickness. Superficial thickness is like a sunburn and affects only the top layer of skin. Partial thickness goes deeper, while full thickness frostbite goes all the

Hypothermia Wrap

1. Place a large ground cloth or tarp flat on the ground.
2. Put a sleeping pad under a sleeping bag in the middle of the tarp.
3. Have your patient get into the bag wearing dry base layers and a warm hat.
4. Place hot-water bottles at the patient's feet, in his groin area, and under his armpits. (Avoid placing the bottles directly against the skin to prevent burning.)
5. Snug up the sleeping bag hood around your patient's face, leaving a small hole for him to see and breathe through. Wrap the ground cloth around the sleeping bag as if you were swaddling a baby, again making sure to leave a space open for his or her face.
6. Keep replacing the water bottles as they cool. Keep your patient wrapped up in this cocoon until he or she returns to normal.

way through the skin into your subcutaneous fat. Full thickness frostbite can cause permanent damage and tissue loss.

Prevention is your best protection against frostbite. Cover your face. Stay hydrated and don't tolerate cold feet or hands. Make it a habit to check your feet routinely. If your toes are numb, stop and take off your boots during the day to warm your feet or change into dry socks. To ensure good circulation, avoid wearing

It's important not to let your feet get too cold in the winter. If you find yourself having trouble warming your feet, ask a friend if you can put them on his or her belly. Skin-to-skin contact is an extremely effective way to warm your feet. DON SHARAF

constricting clothing or too-tight boots. If your toes or fingers get numb, stop and do something. Swing your arms or legs vigorously. If this doesn't work, ask a friend if you can put your cold body part on his or her stomach. It may sound like a big favor, but the skin-to-skin contact is an extremely effective way to warm your feet.

White spots, usually on your nose or cheeks, characterize superficial frostbite, or frostnip. You can rewarm frostnip by holding your hands up to your face and blowing into them. But that is a temporary measure. You'll need to protect your skin from the elements if you want to avoid having the white spots return the minute you lower your hands.

Partial thickness frostbite can be difficult to distinguish from full thickness when it's frozen. The tissue will be pale and feel hard to the touch in either case. In the field, the distinction really doesn't matter. If your tissue is frozen, the question is whether to warm it up so it thaws or wait until you can get to a hospital.

Rewarming is done by submerging the affected part into a warm-water bath (temperature between 104°F and 108°F) until the tissue has thawed. For anyone who has experienced the feeling of the "screaming barfies" as hands or feet rewarm in the winter, you know thawing frostbite is going to be very painful, so be prepared. If you carry any kind of painkillers in your first aid kit, this would be an appropriate time to use them.

The problem with rewarming in the field is that you must keep this bath at 104°–108°F for a long time, which can be difficult if you are out camping. Furthermore, it is imperative that you do not allow the tissue to refreeze after it has thawed, as that can cause more damage. In addition, once the part is thawed, you may not be able to use it because of pain, swelling, and blistering. Because of these factors, you may want to consider keeping the part frozen while you make your way back to civilization.

Immersion Foot

Immersion foot is a nonfreezing cold injury that causes nerve damage and pain. Usually, immersion foot happens in wet environments with temperatures a little above freezing. This becomes a winter hazard when you are out in the fall or spring and temperatures warm during the day.

Classic immersion foot is characterized by mottled, grayish colored feet, but these signs are not always evident. The best way to prevent the condition, therefore, is to recognize the conditions that make it possible and be diligent about keeping your feet warm. This means stopping on the trail to warm your feet if necessary.

Snow Blindness

The glare of the sun off the snow can burn your corneas. The result is pain and light sensitivity that lasts

The glare of the sun off the snow can burn your corneas, causing painful snow blindness. Wear sunglasses or googles to protect your eyes when you are out in the winter. LYNNE WOLFE

for roughly twenty-four hours. Someone with snow blindness can do little more than sit in the dark with damp compresses over her eyes until the pain subsides. The best treatment is avoidance: wear sunglasses even when it's overcast.

Chilblains and Sun Bumps

Our skin can become inflamed in response to extreme cold and sudden warming causing chilblains. Chilblains are characterized by redness, itching, swelling, and blistering and usually occur on your toes, fingers, and nose. Often, you won't notice chilblains until you get home. Symptoms can last a week or two. To prevent chilblains, wear loose-fitting clothing to allow adequate circulation and try not to expose your bare skin to the extreme cold.

Some people develop small blisters or pimples on their skin after exposure to ultraviolet radiation. Sun bumps, as they are called, are common in snowy conditions with intense ultraviolet radiation, and usually occur on people's faces. Sun bumps can be itchy and disfiguring, but tend to go away without treatment after a week or two. The cause of sun bumps is not well understood, but appears to be some kind of reaction to ultraviolet. To prevent sun bumps, wear sun block (zinc oxide and other physical blocks seem to work best) or cover your face with a bandana to keep the sun off.

Raynaud's Syndrome

Raynaud's is a condition that causes the small arteries that supply blood to your skin to spasm in response to cold temperatures and stress, limiting circulation. Typically, Raynaud's occurs in people's fingers or toes. The condition causes skin to turn white, then blue. The affected area feels numb and cold. As the spasms subside, the area may turn red and throb or tingle.

Treatment of Raynaud's depends on its severity. For most people, the problem is more of a nuisance than a disability. Many people know they have Raynaud's before they head out into the winter and have developed tricks for dealing with the problem, such as carrying chemical hand and foot warmers. If you experience an attack of Raynaud's in the field, warm the affected area gently until the spasms subside and circulation improves.

AVALANCHES

This book is not an avalanche manual. It will merely introduce you to the conditions that lead to avalanches so you can evaluate whether it is a hazard you need to be prepared for. If it is, get training. The American Avalanche Institute and the American Institute for Avalanche Research and Education offer courses for beginners through experts. Local ski shops will often host avalanche awareness clinics, or

Even if you are not traveling across a slope steep enough to slide, the runout of an avalanche can travel across low-angle ground. THINKSTOCK.COM, SCUBALUNA

can hook you up with a guide who can lead you safely through avalanche terrain.

Terrain

Slope angle is the most consistent factor in avalanche mechanics. Slab avalanches typically occur on slopes between 30 and 45 degrees, with 38 degrees considered "prime time." Except in extreme wet snow conditions, green light terrain—or slopes under 30 degrees—do not produce avalanches. But if you have steep slopes above you, beware.

The best way to determine slope angle is to use an inclinometer. The perfect avalanche slope

Terrain traps are gullies surrounded by steep slopes where even a small avalanche can bury you. Only travel in terrain traps like this when you know the avalanche hazard is low, such as early morning in the spring when the snow is still frozen. LYNNE WOLFE

is usually also the perfect ski slope, and many of us over or under estimate slope angle based on our skiing expertise. So be conservative and measure the angle before you jump onto it.

Treed slopes can be safer for travel than an open slope, but it depends on the trees. "Unhappy forests," or areas with small, broken, or flagged trees (trees with branches only on the downhill side), are a sign of frequent avalanches. Even widely spaced trees can be deceiving. A good rule of thumb is that trees that are too close together to ski through easily are unlikely to avalanche. This is the best place to put in your travel route.

The small trees at the bottom of this slope, called an "unhappy forest," are clear indicators of frequent avalanches. Before you travel in terrain like this, you must assess conditions to determine if it is safe. MOLLY ABSOLON

Good route finding is critical to safe travel in avalanche country. You should look for ridges, thick trees, and low angle slopes when choosing your path. Avoid gullies or terrain traps where even a small slide can pile up deeply. Know what is above you. If you cannot see because of weather or trees, read a map. Avalanches sweeping down from above have caught many winter travelers unaware.

If you find yourself forced to cross potentially hazardous terrain, cross one at a time. Post spotters in islands of safety and watch each other cross. If the slope avalanches, you can mark the last scene spot for your companion. This can shave precious time off your search by narrowing down your options.

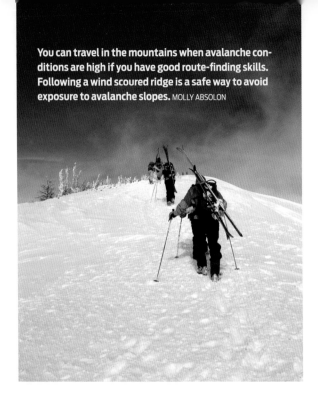

You can travel in the mountains when avalanche conditions are high if you have good route-finding skills. Following a wind scoured ridge is a safe way to avoid exposure to avalanche slopes. MOLLY ABSOLON

Weather

Most avalanches occur during or right after storms that bring 6 or more inches of snow. Remember, wind can transport snow, so a storm that drops only 3 inches but is blowing at 25 mph can be loading leeward slopes and increasing the avalanche hazard.

After storms, look around for signs of recent avalanche activity. If you see slides, you can expect there to be others on similar aspects at the same elevation. Dig into the snowpack to see how the new snow is reacting.

Storms that come in cold and warm up increase the avalanche hazard because they create what is called an "upside down" snowpack, with heavier snow on top of light, cold powder. So pay attention to the temperature during a storm cycle.

Snowpack

Analyzing the snowpack is the most complex part of avalanche forecasting.

You need two things in your snowpack to create a slab avalanche: a cohesive slab of snow and a weak sliding layer. The best way to know if these two

To truly know what is going on in the snowpack, you need to dig down and look. This photo shows a large surface hoar crystal that formed on top of the snow during a clear, cold spell. When surface hoar like this gets buried, it becomes a dangerous sliding layer. MOLLY ABSOLON

conditions exist is to pay attention to the snowpack throughout the season. Avalanche forecasts will give you information about general conditions in the area. Most mountainous parts of the world have an avalanche hotline or website that gives daily forecasts, as well as historical data on the snowpack and recent avalanche activity. But remember, these forecasts are general and do not guarantee you safety. You need to evaluate the conditions where you are in conjunction with the information you glean from the forecast.

Snow pits are another way to see what's going on beneath your feet. Dig down at least 4 feet or so and look at the layers.

Snowpack analysis is challenging for beginners, and a book is not the place to learn about it. Take an avalanche course if you think you want to be out on slopes that can slide. Travel with more knowledgeable friends and have them explain why and how they are making their decisions. Look for signs: broken-off trees, old avalanches, changing temperatures, rapid snow accumulation, whumpfing snow, and high winds are just some of the warning signs that conditions could be deteriorating, and the avalanche hazard increasing.

Safety Equipment

Travelers in avalanche terrain should be equipped with a shovel, an avalanche transceiver, and a probe. These pieces of equipment allow you to find and dig out your partners in the event of an avalanche. Without them, you may end up simply standing by while someone you care about dies.

Carrying safety equipment is useless, however, if you don't know how to use it. Practice searching with your transceiver and digging up buried backpacks, so you are ready if the worst should occur.

There are other specialized pieces of avalanche equipment, such as the AvaLung or an airbag backpack, available on the market. These things are designed to improve your survivability if you are caught in an avalanche. Skiers, snowboarders, and mountaineers use them when they enter terrain they know can avalanche.

ICE

Frozen rivers, lakes, and streams can be great places to travel, or they can be extremely dangerous if the ice is not strong enough to support your weight.

Here are a few things to consider when evaluating the safety of ice:

» Rocks, stumps, and other objects sticking up out of the ice can trap heat, making the ice in that area thinner and weaker.

» Areas where there is current tend to have thinner ice, so avoid inlets and outlets to lakes, the outside of bends, or places where the gradient of a stream steepens.

In midwinter, traveling across frozen lakes can be fast and easy, but as the ice melts, beware. Lake outlets, rivers with a lot of current, and places where objects stick out tend to melt out fastest, making travel hazardous. MOLLY ABSOLON

A thick layer of snow on a frozen lake insulates its surface, preventing a thick layer of ice from forming underneath.

If you decide the ice is safe, cross on skis or snowshoes, so your weight is spread out over a larger area. Use your ski pole to tap the ice ahead of you. A solid thunk should be a reassuring sound. A hollow sound can mean thinner ice, so be cautious. Spread your group out.

If you do fall through the ice, the critical thing, according to Dr. Gordon Giesbrecht, the director of the University of Manitoba's Laboratory for Exercise and Environmental Medicine, is to avoid panic. You can watch a great video of him talking about this while submerged in an icy bath on the *Late Show with David Letterman* on YouTube.

Giesbrecht has an expression that can save your life if you find yourself submerged: "One minute, ten minutes, one hour."

In the first minute, your body panics in response to the shock of the cold water. Your best bet during this time is to try to relax and to wait for your breathing to stabilize as your body adjusts. Once that minute passes, you have 10 minutes of functional movement, during which you should try to get out of the water. The best technique is to extend your arms across the ice and kick, trying to push yourself up onto the ice. If this works, you'll end up lying on the surface. Stay prone and pull yourself across to thicker ice or the shore before trying to stand.

If you cannot get out, don't give up. Giesbrecht says humans can live a long time in cold water. You have about an hour before you will lose consciousness, but even then people can survive much longer, as long as they do not drown. To avoid drowning, keep your arms extended on the ice. Your hope is that they will freeze in place, securing you to the ice even if you lose consciousness.

If a member of your party falls into the ice, do not try to approach. Find a long stick or a rope that you can throw or extend across the ice to your colleague. Make a loop in the rope that he can put it over his head and under his arms, so you can pull him out. Stay a long way back from the broken ice to ensure the safety of the rest of the party.

Chapter Six
Closing Thoughts

Sometimes reading a book about winter camping, with all its warnings and caveats, can be intimidating rather than inspiring. No doubt winter camping is hard and takes commitment, but the rewards are huge.

You may find yourself watching an ermine skitter across a glittering meadow, or you may come upon tracks that tell a story of some animal's passing. You may enjoy perfect powder on an untracked slope

It's easy to avoid getting out in the winter. It's cold, you need a lot of stuff, and it's hard work, but the rewards are well worth the effort. ALLEN O'BANNON

The beauty of the winter world is inspiring. It's worth the work getting out there. AJ LINNELL

miles from anyone else, or you may be awed by the beauty of a snow-covered forest. The feeling of being out in the winter is invigorating and a good counter to the cabin fever that descends on us all after a long, dark winter cooped up inside.

So don't let the challenges keep you at home. Start small. Go with friends who can teach you. Have a contingency plan if things don't turn out the way you plan. And have fun.

Index